Top 3 Online Learning Platforms: Dissected

The purpose of this section is to give you an understanding of the Top 3 Online Learning platforms: Coursera, edX, and Udacity. This is not going to be like the free articles you see everywhere that claim to compare the three, and sometimes even try to give them a "score", but by then end of the article the writer just, "But really it's up to your learning style". We're going to go deep. We're going to actually figure out which platform is right for you, and you'll leave this section with a good idea of where to start.

Keep in mind, online classes aren't the best for everyone. In fact, we have another section called "Self Taught vs. Online Classes: The Ultimate Guide" that helps you figure out which path is right for you. This section assumes that you've already read "Self-Taught vs. Online Classes: The Ultimate Guide" and have decided that online learning is best for you. All of that said, online classes are a great tool to beef up your data skills, and even if it's not the end-all-be-all, you'll probably find yourself taking courses at some point, even if it's just to supplement your self-study.

Let's begin by thinking about the outcome for you taking the course. Naturally everyone wants to learn, but there are other factors as well that need to be weighed, which will ultimately affect your decision. Here are some things to consider:

What type of role are you interested in? What path in data is best for you? If you're not sure, try reading (or re-reading) the chapter, "Discover Your Path in Data" and find roles that are right for you.

What is your current level of skill? Are you starting from scratch, or do you have some experience writing SQL, Python, doing data analysis, maybe even statistics, etc? Most platforms have options for all levels, but it's good to think about where you stand as you evaluate different resources.

Are you looking to get a credential or certificate of some sort, or is just the knowledge enough for you? If you're interested in a credential, is there additional value to you in having a University attached to it? Most candidates are interested in having something certifiable to show that they've completed the course and learned the material.

How much are you willing to invest in a course? Don't worry if you're not able to invest a lot- most people can't. There are free and low-priced options for educating yourself online. If you do have a budget, however, more power to you, and you may be able to get more of the "premium" learning experiences.

Going back to the idea of your outcome, what is yours? We want to get specific here, and make it exciting. "I want to learn data science" is not a good outcome. First of all, it's not specific enough for you to understand when you've achieved the outcome. How do you know when you've "learned data science"? We can do better than that.

How about, "My outcome is to develop skills in data science that enable me to get a role as a Data Scientist at a tech company. In particular, I want to focus on machine learning and be competent at producing useful models." This is much better because it's exact enough to let you know where you stand. You can take some time to aggregate job postings for data scientists and list out the skills you see come up regularly, then self-assess as you learn new concepts. For example, maybe "linear regression" is listed on several Data Scientist role postings, so you can work on that skill and evaluate yourself.

Our second version is good, but it still needs a little work. It needs to be more inspiring. Language is very impactful for us, and having a juicy outcome will push you to do better than your best and will motivate you to navigate through setbacks. Remember this: what you say matters, and how you say it matters. We've covered the what (be specific, etc.), and now we're going to work on the "how to say it".

Try saying this outcome out loud, with lots of energy: "My outcome is to create and cultivate top-level skills that help me get a fantastic job as a Data Scientist at a great company where I'd be excited to come into work every day."

Isn't that sexier than, "I want to learn data science"? You bet it is. This is the kind of outcome that inspires and motivates you to do incredible work and improve yourself at a lightening-fast rate. This is the kind of outcome that gets you to jump out of bed at 4am on Saturday with a huge smile on your face, ready to take on the world and get to work on your skills. This is the type of outcome that makes you hungry for knowledge. This outcome gives you drive. When it comes to taking online classes, everyone has moments when they don't want to watch the lecture, don't want to take notes, don't want to do the assignment right now, etc. Everyone has moments where they'd rather watch TV or go get something to eat or hang out with friends. When this happens to you and you're feeling demotivated, a juicy outcome will pump you up and get you back in the zone to do great work.

Now, write out your outcome. Make it specific, and make it interesting. Make it juicy. This is going to carry you through the inevitable challenges that arise when you're trying to break into a new field. Your outcome is essentially a reminder to yourself of what, exactly, you want, and it will help you understand if you're heading in the right direction or not. Keep in mind, it's flexible too- for example, you may initially write as a part of your outcome that you want to work at a top 10 tech company, but later discover that you're actually interested in the idea of a smaller company, in which case it's absolutely fine to update your outcome. Know where you're going, and be flexible in your approach. This is going to be your North Star.

Now, we can get to the meat of this section: understanding the top 3 online learning platforms and helping you understand which one will best help you reach your outcome. It is important to think about this up front, before you invest time and money because you want to ensure that you're making the most of your resources (again, time and money). Make sure to read this section all the way through before starting a course or putting in your credit card info anywhere.

We're going to evaluate these platforms using 3 Cs: Coursework, Credentialing, and Cost. Sections on Coursework will help you understand what types of things you can learn on the given platform, which is a major factor in choosing which direction to go. Credentialing will cover what sort of certifications are available. All of these platforms offer some sort of credential, but they vary in subtle ways that can impact your path (if credentialing is an important factor to you).

We'll also cover costs and give you a good idea of what sort of investment is required, if any. The price structure for most online education platforms is usually that courses are free to try or perhaps fully audit, but paying unlocks premium content and credentials/certificates. The good news is that you can learn almost anything for free online, so there are options for every budget, including $0. At this point, cost should be the least of your concerns, but we'll make sure to get you fully up to speed.

    We'll be sure to point out any subtle differences between the platforms and try to give you an understanding of what the user experience will be like. Additionally, after we go over each platform in detail, we'll dissect factors like cost and credentialing further to answer questions like, "Do I even need an official certificate?" Again, make sure to read through this entire section before making a decision and moving forward with an online learning platform. Let's begin.

Udacity
udacity.com

Udacity was founded in 2011 by Sebastian Thrun, a former Vice President at Google and Professor of Computer Science at Stanford. Depending on your age, you may remember that back in 2011 Stanford open-sourced some of its courses in Computer Science, and those courses were actually the starting point for Udacity. Here's their mission statement: "Our mission is to democratize education through the offering of world-class higher education opportunities that are accessible, flexible, and economical."

Udacity is a great platform and definitely one of the most popular among online learners, even those who traditionally have self-taught.

Coursework

Udacity has a great deal of coursework available, neatly organized into categories like, "Data Science" or, "Artificial Intelligence". Interestingly, within categories, the coursework is sometimes subdivided into job titles such as "Data Analyst" or "Data Engineer", which are often referring to Udacity's Nanodegrees, which are just what the name implies- small versions of degrees that focus on one particular skillset (e.g. Data Analytics) and have several courses teaching different concepts.

Outside of the bread-and-butter coursework for something like a Data Analyst path, Udacity offers other interesting subjects for study. For example, they have a great body of classes on Autonomous Systems, including coursework on Self-Driving technology and Robotics. For someone who already has a great technical base and is looking to branch into more advanced coursework, there are a lot of compelling options.

Additionally there are some courses available to help you along with your career, including a class called, "Applying for Jobs", and one called, "Interviewing". Since you should already have our other section, "6 Figures in 60 Days: The Ultimate Strategy", you should be OK on this topic, but some people feel more comfortable supplementing their knowledge and hearing another voice. If that describes you, feel free to make use of these Udacity offerings, but keep in mind that early in your journey you want to establish a solid foundation of technical and problem-solving skills, which means your time is best spent learning the ins and outs of how to work with data effectively.

Overall, Udacity has a great body of coursework, but is somewhat limited compared to other platforms (meaning there are fewer course options). One interesting part of Udacity is that there tends to be just one course (or very few) on a specific topic. For example, there's just one course on Data Visualization with Python. As we'll see later in this chapter, other platforms often offer multiple courses on the same (or similar) subjects, usually with a different teacher. This tells us that Udacity has taken a curated approach to creating their catalog, which has its pros and cons.

The upsides of this approach include the fact that it's much easier to choose coursework on Udacity than other platforms, if you've already determined what path is right for you. For example, let's say you want to ultimately be a Data Engineer- there's basically one choice on Udacity: the Data Engineer Nanodegree. This is a benefit for most people because many get lost in, "analysis paralysis", which is when you have so many options that you're just overwhelmed and don't end up choosing anything at all. That is not a place you want to be (trust me).

The downsides of having one or few options is that there really isn't a way to re-adjust if you're not getting in sync with the instructor or the way the material is presented. As you surely remember from high school, different teachers work better or worse with different students, and a lot of it comes down to the style of the teacher and how they arrange the coursework. That said, this shouldn't be a major concern, for two reasons: 1. Udacity offers a refund if you cancel within the first 7 days of starting a Nanodegree, and 2. Instructors on this and other top platforms are vetted and have shown that they can effectively teach the material. When using a major online learning platform like Udacity, most people find they succeed if they put in the time and effort to do well.

Credentialing

Now, let's get into the credentialing/certification options available. Udacity has carved out its own place in this space through "Nanodegree" programs. A Nanodegree is an earned credential signifying that you've met a certain standard of learning set forth by the Nanodegree program. This is the same idea as other certificates that exist, such as the PMP certification for project managers (Project Management Professional) or Six Sigma certification for those involved in improving business processes.

Some platforms offer certificates for single courses, but Nanodegrees are earned only through completion of an entire set of coursework. For example, in order to earn a Nanodegree in Data Science, you'd have to complete all of the courses in the Data Scientist program. This is great for learners who aren't already familiar with exactly what subject matter they need to learn.

Cost

First, let's get an understanding of the free options available to you Udacity, as well as the limitations of the free options. Udacity offers a number of full courses free-of-charge, and there are some very useful ones such as, "Intro to Relational Databases" and "A/B Testing" (statistics). These are great for brushing up on foundational concepts or specific skills that complement other learning material.

The downside of these free courses is that there's not really a logical learning structure the course fits into. In the example of the A/B Testing course, you can definitely take it and learn useful material, but how do you know where it fits into the grand scheme of your potential role? Is it even information you need to focus on for your specific path in data and the roles you're applying to? Knowing about A/B testing certainly wouldn't hurt, but there are a lot of data roles that don't need to have an in-depth knowledge of how to execute these tasks.

Additionally, most of the coursework with the Nanodegree learning programs isn't offered for free. For example, signing up for the Data Engineer Nanodegree and paying the monthly fee will unlock lots of great courses and content that just isn't accessible for free. One of the main advantages of full online learning programs, as opposed to just one-off courses, is that you're learning something end-to-end, and thinks link together in a coherent way. You start out with foundational information, ie. things you need to know that make it possible to learn everything else. Then, you get into more specific information, but you do so in a fluid way- everything connects and it helps your comprehension dramatically.

If you're looking to brush up on some specific skills, and Udacity has a course on that subject, go ahead and stick with the free version. If you're looking for something more complete and comprehensive, you'll probably want to go with the paid Nanodegree programs or choose a different platform.

Before we move on to a detailed explanation of the paid programs Udacity offers, there's one thing we should call out- the, "Career Advancement" courses. These are video lectures that aren't focused on the technical side of being a professional in data- instead, these courses deal with soft skills that are essential to being successful in any data path long-term. Regardless of where you are in your career, you should definitely go through the courses related to interviews if you're looking for a new job (eg., "Data Science Interviews"). We'll give you some great advice in these chapters, and there are plenty of resources out there, but definitely check these out too.

The costs associated with learning programs on Udacity are fairly straightforward. For a Nanodegree, the cost as of this writing is $399 per month, and programs range from 2-6 months in length. There is also the option of paying up-front for the coursework and getting a decent discount. Here's the current cost breakdowns for the three paths we've discussed in this book:

Data Analyst (est. 4 months): $399/mo = $1,596 total, or $1,436 if paid up front.

Data Scientist (est. 4 months): $399/mo = $1,596 total, or $1,436 if paid up front.

Data Engineer (est. 5 months): $399/mo = $1,995 total, or $1,795 if paid up front.

As you can see, there's the opportunity to save a little money if you decide to pay up front. Before you charge your credit card, there's something you should keep in mind: no matter what the estimated program length is, you don't have to pay once you're done with the curriculum.

For example, let's say you start the Data Scientist program and work your tail off to finish in 2.5 months. You would only pay for 3 months (you're billed on the first and there's no partial-month billing), which would come to a total of $1,197 ($399 * 3). This obviously beats the discount price. The other thing to note is that even if you do the "paid up front" option, you'll only get access for the number of months they estimate it will take you to finish the curriculum, and if you need more time you'll have to start paying $399 per month. In other words, paying up front isn't a way to insure that you'll get a lower rate if you need more time to finish.

If you're the type of person who is going to work like crazy on the online courses and really spend time focused on learning the material, it's probably better to go with the monthly payments and see if you can finish early. On the other hand, if you lots of other obligations that mean you won't be able to give this a ton of time, and think that you'll probably complete the courses in the estimated time or longer, you might want to go ahead and pay up front.

That said, if you're unsure about where you stand, we recommend paying monthly and really giving this your best effort. $399 is a big chunk of money for most people, and seeing that CC charge every month should motivate you to work hard and push through the coursework to completion.

Lastly in this section, we want to remind you should take your time to think about your options before investing in online coursework. You need to understand what path you're going to take, what skills you have, what skills you need, and how important the credentialing aspect is to you. We're going to address some of the nuance here in later sections, but don't let these numbers make you too nervous or get you too excited- be patient and try to figure out what's right for you. Udacity and other online learning platforms are fantastic resources, and they're often even better when you pay for premium versions, but remember that you don't have to invest a lot of money (or any money) into learning these skills to be successful. Just about anything can be learned online for free, and ultimately what will get you a great role and move your career forward are real skills to do the work.

edX
edX.org

    Another popular online learning platform is edX, which was founded in 2012 by the Massachusetts Institute of Technology (M.I.T.) and Harvard University. EdX has goals similar to Udacity, but one of the key differences is that all of the course content is provided by actual universities and higher-education institutions. Does this matter? Maybe, maybe not, but it might be beneficial to receive instruction from people who have been teaching for a long time and have plenty of practice communicating the concepts. Also, there is the fact that you can attach the name of the institution when you put your coursework on your resume, but we'll go over that in more detail in the, "Credentialing" section.

Also, know that edX is a non-profit (hence the .org domain name). This probably doesn't mean much in practice, but some people feel better taking classes through non-profit organizations over for-profit companies.

Coursework

EdX coursework is largely provided by the institutions themselves. One of the interesting features of edX coursework is that they offer much more subject matter variety than platforms like Udacity, which focus on technical skills. EdX has a multitude of offerings in not only Data and Computer Science, but also subjects like Entrepreneurship, Chemistry, Math, and Medicine (and many more).

But you want to learn about data and acquire the skills to get you a fantastic new role, so does this matter? For most, no, but for people who are in no rush to move into a new career path and want to build foundational, theory-level skills, courses like "Fundamentals of Statistics", "Statistical Thinking for Data Science", or "Essential Math for Machine Learning" could be really useful.

Either way, you can still leverage the courses in Data on edX to help you achieve your goals. EdX actually has more ways than most major platforms to learn important material: individual courses, Professional Certificates, MicroMasters, Online Master's, and XSeries. What do all of these mean? Let's look at short descriptions of each and make the picture clear.

Individual Courses: Pretty self-explanatory. These come in many different flavors, with courses such as "Data Science: Visualization", or "Python Basics for Data Science". Most of the courses allow you to take them for free, and pay extra if you'd like to have your assignments graded and receive an official certificate of completion. This is a major advantage over Udacity, which does offer some free courses, but likely not as much as most people are looking for.

Professional Certificates: These are interesting groups of coursework that are comprised of several related courses that combine nicely to build your skills in a certain area. One good example is the, "Microsoft Professional Program in Artificial Intelligence" (created by Microsoft, of course). These are nice because you'll get a more coherent body of information than you would semi-randomly selecting courses. The downside is that these tend to be pretty narrow in focus, so if you're looking to build a more end-to-end skillset it may be better to go with a different option. You can take individual courses for free, or pay per course and get the certifiable certificate.

MicroMasters: As you can see, the good people at edX are quite creative with their program creation. Jokes aside, a MicroMasters could be an interesting route for someone looking to get into the field of data and may want to get a Master's degree in the future. Essentially a MicroMasters is a group of connected courses that are the fundamental courses you would take in a Master's program. The MicroMasters stands on its own like any other certificate, and if you choose to go for a full Master's degree in the future you can get those course credits applied to your degree (you won't have to pay for them again or take the courses again). For example, you could sign up for the MicroMasters program in Data Science from the University of San Diego, and then later get your full Master's in Data Science. Make sure you read the fine print if you're going to pursue this route, however, because MicroMasters coursework for a given program only applies to one (or a select few) universities.

MicroMaster programs will take a bit longer than other certificates, and edX estimates around 1 year to complete the full program.

Online Master's Degrees: We're seeing a somewhat new area emerge in the world of online learning- true Master's Degrees, fully online. Curriculum-wise these are no different than a Master's you would earn by attending a university on-campus, but there are a few key advantages: they're fully online, they're somewhat self-paced in that you can take however many classes per semester that fit into your schedule, and they often cost less than a traditional on-campus program. These are the most in-depth option into the subject matter and will likely take students 1-3 years to complete, depending on your course load. We'll talk more about credentialing in the next section, but as you can imagine, a Master's degree makes it easy for recruiters and hiring managers to understand your level of knowledge. Note that these are actual degrees offered by universities such as Georgia Tech and the University of Texas, so you would have a degree from the university, not edX.

XSeries: Yes, another program type offered by edX. Once again these are sponsored by institutions, and the main difference is these are a bit more focused on the application of skills to a particular field or industry, and are generally more in-depth than other course offerings. For example, one program is called, "Data Analysis for Life

Sciences". Other than that, the format is fairly similar, with the programs usually having around four courses and estimated to take 4-6 months of effort. As of this writing, XSeries is the most limited option with fewer than five programs focused on data, so it may be best to go with one of the above options.

So, what should you pick? Again, don't sign up for anything until you've read this section in full, but by now you're probably getting an idea of what's right for you. Most people, regardless of their work experience, find that program-based online learning helps them move closer to their goal of getting a great job in data than taking individual courses, which are usually better suited for people who are already in a data-driven role and want to beef up their skills.

Another important consideration is the time you're willing to spend on coursework. Do you want to take a few years and get your Master's? What about one year? Many people want to spend just a few months on a program, get out in the job market, land a job, and then improve their skills from there. Keep in mind that a longer program isn't necessarily better and won't necessarily get you a better job.

Credentialing

Thankfully, edX credentials are somewhat easier to understand than the program structure itself. You have a lot of options, so when it comes to credentials it's best to think about them in terms of four buckets: Professional Certificates, MicroMasters, Master's Degrees, and no credential at all. Let's look at each one in detail.

Profession Certificates are offered at just about every online learning platform that exists, and edX is no different. One interesting contrast between edX and Udacity is that, with edX, you can get a certificate for a single course, whereas with Udacity the only certification comes with taking a full Nanodegree. Most learners pursue fuller program-time online education, but this is something to be aware of.

Another interesting distinction with edX compared to many other platforms is that the content is sponsored by a university or institution, rather than the platform itself- meaning, of course, that you'd have a certificate that looks something like, "Professional Certificate in Data Science from Harvard" rather than, "from edX" (although certificates themselves are co-branded with both the sponsoring institution and edX.

VERIFIED
CERTIFICATE of ACHIEVEMENT

This is to certify that

David J. Malan
Gordon McKay Professor
of the Practice of Computer Science
Harvard University

John Harvard

successfully completed and received a passing grade in

CS50: Introduction to Computer Science

a course of study offered by HarvardX, an online learning initiative of Harvard University through edX.

VERIFIED CERTIFICATE
Issued January 12, 2017

VALID CERTIFICATE ID
ae8f7145d7084dc8a12c6ea0d8d1559d

Why is this an important distinction? Many believe that having a university brand on a resume carries a bit more weight than just an online learning platform, since it's possible that there is still some stigma around online learning, and it's almost certainly true that a top university wouldn't risk its reputation with educational material of sub-par value. Plus, if the course content came from a university like Harvard or Berkeley, it's easier for recruiters and hiring managers to trust the quality of what you were taught. Think about it- if you have a Professional Certificate in Data Science from Harvard, as a hiring manager I would have more confidence in that educational material than an online platform without the same reputation. If you had a certificate from Never-heard-of-it.com, the hiring manager wouldn't have a clue if you'd been taught that 2 + 2 = 5 or the sky is green, or worse. The general recommendation we give to people is to go for online learning programs that have the content created by universities or reputable companies, rather than the platforms themselves.

MicroMasters are the next evolution of online learning. For these, obviously you'll need to take an entire program to get the credential, rather than just a single course, and naturally these are sponsored by universities and other educational institutions. As we mentioned before, these are fantastic if you're interested in getting a Master's degree at some point but don't want to make the full leap just yet, but the question remains of whether these are a "better" credential than a Professional Certificate.

Opinions are mixed. On the one hand, some people (including some hiring managers and recruiters) see no difference, since both program types involve online learning and likely have similar content. On the other hand, some people perceive a MicroMasters as more valuable since the courses are true graduate-level courses and apply toward a Master's degree at the given institution. In other words, it goes without saying that these classes aren't a walk in the park. In the end, the choice of Professional Certificate vs. MicroMasters will come down to what kind of information you want to learn (there are generally more options in the Professional Certificate group), what kind of time and financial commitment you're willing to make, and what you think the future holds for you and the type of education you want to pursue.

The last program type we'll discuss in the Credential section is also the easiest for everyone to understand: the Master's Degree. On edX, Master's degrees are just that- a Master's in the program of study from the given institution. These degrees should pass any educational background check and won't look any different than if you got your Master's on campus. For most learners and job seekers, it's a no-brainer that they'd prefer to get a Master's degree than anything else, and it's probably true that it holds more weight than any other certification. In the wide, wide world of credentialing, the Master's wins, but more often than not people chose to pursue a different route for two main reasons: time and cost. We've already talked about the time commitment in the above section describing the coursework, and we'll talk about cost in the next section. Just know that if you're looking to invest a few years and $10k+ on education in the data world, a Master's degree is probably right for you, and edX has some great ones to choose from.

Thoughts from a Hiring Manager:

"I don't know a lot about online programs or the differences between them. The reason I think completing online coursework is great is it shows me the person is committed to improving themselves and willing to put in the work to get better. On the other hand, I also know that online learning has its disadvantages, and a certificate or something is no guarantee the candidate actually knows the information. Of course I would give a candidate with online learning the same technical and business case questions I give everyone, and really try to get a thorough understanding of what they can do and how well they'd fit into the role."

My advice for anyone looking to pursue online learning is to do it for the right reasons: namely, that you want to learn skills to do great work. The wrong reason would be that you want a credential on your resume. The credential may get you interviews at some companies, but a credential alone won't get you a job, and it certainly won't make you successful once you do get a job.

Cost

At last, the question that's probably been on your mind while reading this section: how much does all this cost? It varies by the type of program. In general edX online programs are less expensive than Udacity's, which (combined with the university name brands) makes for a compelling offer for those looking to break into the data world.

One other important point of comparison is the availability of the materials as it relates to the cost. As we saw in the last section, Udacity's Nanodegree programs require a paid monthly subscription to not only receive the official certificate, but also to access the material at all. Many people love edX because they can access the course material for free, and only if they want a verified certificate do they have to pay anything. Not that this is true for a large majority of the coursework on edX, but curriculum in the Online Master's programs will likely not be available.

Here's a closer look at the costs for the programs mentioned:

Individual courses: Once again, these are fairly limited in scope but can be great resources for digging into a specific topic. For example, "Essential Math for Machine Learning: Python Edition" is currently offered through Microsoft, and would be very useful for those looking to pursue Data Science roles involving algorithms and machine learning. If you'd like a verified certificate, the cost is $99.

Professional Certificate: The next level up, the Professional Certificate, involves much more comprehensive coursework and essentially strings together relevant material that will help you build holistic skills in a given area. Another offering from Microsoft is the, "Microsoft Professional Program in Data Science". This has ten courses and a capstone project (which counts as a course), and you can get the official program certificate for $99 per course, or $1,089. As of the time of this writing there doesn't appear to be a discount for purchasing the whole program. Most other Professional Certificates are in this price range, with individual courses typically costing $99.

MicroMasters: This is where the cost structure starts to change a bit. The price will depend on the program and university, but for something in a data career path you can expect to pay somewhere between $1,000-$1,500 for four courses. Note that while there are far fewer classes to take, these real, graduate-level courses with plenty of substance to challenge you and help you grow. Another thing to note is that, while you can buy these courses individually, some programs do give you a discount for purchasing the whole MicroMasters at once. For example, the University of San Diego Data Science MicroMasters currently costs $350 for individual courses, but if you the whole program together (4 courses), you only pay $1,260, which saves you $___ (you do the calculation- you're in the data world now).

It's worth pointing out that MicroMasters are interesting because, while they aren't technically college credit, they can be applied to a Master's degree in the future, which makes them a lot more valuable for those who want to pursue even higher education later on.

Online Master's Degrees: Pull your wallet out for this one- an online Master's through edX will cost you somewhere from $9,000-$15,000, depending on which data program you choose. While the cost here is definitely a long way from the Professional Certificates and even MicroMasters, many people (including recruiters and hiring managers) believe that this is the most legitimate and comprehensive form of online learning. It's certainly worth considering, but remember that plenty of people have outstanding careers in data without a postgraduate degree, and at even some of the most prestigious tech companies you're likely to find that the majority of successful data analysts, scientists, and engineers don't have a Master's.

All of that said, consider it. If this is an area where you're willing to invest the time and money required to get a Master's, you'll probably enjoy it and learn an incredible amount of useful information and skills that will put you on the path to long-term success.

XSeries: In the final program offering, we're circling back to the first pricing model we saw: roughly $99 per course. XSeries clock in at 3-4 courses, so you're looking at $300-$400 for a certificate. The selection for edX's XSeries programs is quite limited, and in conversations with both people looking to break into data and those already in the field who want to improve their skills we've found that there's not as much interest in XSeries. Take a look at the courses for yourself and see if any of the programs make sense for your goals.

coursera

Coursera
coursera.com

    Coursera is another major online learning platform that is an offshoot of online coursework at Stanford, founded by former professors Andrew Ng and Daphne Koller. If you've done the research on online learning in the data world before, you've probably heard of founder Andrew Ng- his seminal online course in Machine Learning is widely considered as one of the most important efforts in the establishment of online learning as a legitimate way to build crucial job skills.

    Coursera is a massive platform, and as of this writing over 40 million people have taken courses here. Undoubtedly you've explored or at least heard about this platform before, so let's get into the details and see if it makes sense for you.

Coursework

Like edX, coursework on Coursera is backed by universities and other institutions. The University of Michigan, Johns Hopkins, IBM, and many international universities are among the institutions that create and support course content. If you decide to pursue a program through Coursera, you'll find that the majority of the classes are taught by professors or other leaders at the institutions themselves.

What's impressive and really stands out about Coursera is the breadth and depth of offerings available in the data world, and while browsing through the site you definitely get the feeling that it's a data-oriented platform. In addition to straightforward programs such as, "Data Science" (by Johns Hopkins), there are also deep dives into fascinating topics, such as the "Deep Learning Specialization", offered by deeplearning.ai, a company that has made it its mission to make education in Artificial Intelligence available to people around the world.

Fortunately, Coursera has taken a more simplified approach to program types than edX, but has a little more flexibility than Udacity. Let's dig into each offering and get to know the intricacies.

Individual Courses: Like our other platforms, Coursera offers individual courses in data-related subjects, such as "The Data Scientist's Toolbox", or "Python Data Structures". You can take these for free, or elect to pay a fee and get an official certificate of completion. Note that individual courses are almost always a part of a larger program called a Specialization, and the cost structure doesn't change much- most learners find themselves just enrolling in the Specialization and taking whichever courses they want.

Specializations: This is Coursera's bread and butter- the specialization. These are groups of ~4-6 courses that are designed to build foundational knowledge in the topic at hand. For example, one of Coursera's most popular Specializations is, "Applied Data Science with Python", offered by the University of Michigan. This particular program has four courses, and starts with the basics of Python programming and data manipulation, and gradually works you up to Machine Learning and Text Mining in later courses.

Specializations are roughly the equivalent of Professional Certificates from edX, and similar to Nanodegrees from Udacity (although the total courseload may be different). Learners and job seekers love Coursera's specializations in part because they do a nice job at being detailed and specific enough to be useful, but broad enough to provide good fundamental knowledge in Data Science, Analytics, or Engineering.

Thoughts from a Data Professional

"I had done some data work before- Excel, super basic SQL, and even taught myself some Python. I tried some sites like Codecademy and DataQuest to try to get the skills to become a Data Scientist, but neither really gave me the foundational knowledge I knew I needed. I signed up for Coursera and realized I love the part-lecture, part-interactive format of the specializations. It took a lot of work and personal drive to not only complete the courses, but actually learn the material, but it was worth it in the end- I finished my specialization in Data Science and eventually landed a job as a Data Scientist at my dream tech company in San Francisco."

Bachelor's & Master's Degrees: Coursera has helped build some highly-rated degree offerings, including both Master's and Bachelor's degrees. At the time of this writing the only data-specific degrees are Master's, while the more technical Bachelor's degrees are in Computer Science, but it's worth noting as you scope out options in the future.

There are only a few Master's degree options, but Coursera is expanding continuously and is looking to add more options. As we mentioned before, Master's Degrees are probably seen as the most legitimate online learning, but also take more time and require a larger financial investment. Also, as of now, Master's Degrees on Coursera are more expensive than those offered by edX, but we'll look more closely at this in the Cost section.

MasterTrack: Somewhat newer in the Coursera portfolio of options is the MasterTrack, which is similar to what we saw from edX in that you can take groups of courses from a particular institution, and if you later decide to enroll in their Master's program you will be able to apply that work to your degree. As of this writing there are only four MasterTrack programs, and neither of the two data-oriented programs are currently active (although it seems they'll be active soon).

One important thing to note as you review your options on Coursera: read the fine print and don't any assumptions about coursework applying to degrees. MasterTrack programs are intended to help you make progress toward an advanced degree, but currently Specializations do not contribute to a Master's (or Bachelor's). For example, Coursera offers a Master's in Applied Data Science through the University of Michigan, and there is also a Specialization in Applied Data Science through the University of Michigan. Although some of the coursework is likely to be similar, coursework in the Specialization would not apply to the degree. That said, it would definitely help you to understand the material and succeed, and it's likely they would take your completion of the Specialization into account when reviewing your application to the Master's program.

Credential

This section will be pretty simple, as the credentialing process is similar to what we saw in the edX portion of this chapter. Let's take a look at each program offering and compare:

Individual Courses: Should you choose to sign up for a paid Coursera subscription, you'll receive an official certificate of completion upon finishing a course. The interesting thing here is that, in order to take an individual course, you usually have to sign up for the Specialization the course is a part of. From there you're free to bounce around and take whichever courses you choose, and it won't affect how much you ultimately pay.

Specializations: Subscribing to Coursera comes with the obvious benefit of receiving a verifiable certificate of completion for the Specialization- for example, the

"Specialization in Applied Data Science" from the University of Michigan. As you can imagine, the certificate itself is co-branded with both Coursera and the sponsoring institution:

One of our student's Specialization Certificate (she got a great job as a Data Scientist)

One unique thing to note is that, while you will receive a certificate of completion for the whole Specialization, you'll also receive certificates for each individual course along the way. Does this matter?

Probably not for most people, but in the event your studies get interrupted it may be nice to have certificates for the courses your were able to complete.

Bachelor's & Master's Degrees: No surprise here- a degree is a degree. Any degree you complete from Coursera will be the same as a degree you complete on campus, be it from the University of Michigan or the Imperial College of London. These are true degrees and carry weight in the job market, but come only through a hefty investment of both time and money.

Those interested in pursuing an advanced degree should take time to weigh the pros and cons wisely, and it is probably beneficial to audit a Specialization through the same institution to see if the coursework interests you enough to spend 1-3 years studying it in a degree program, as well as if you like the format of online learning. Also, some learners consider getting a Bachelor's in a technical field, rather than pursuing a Master's. If you don't currently have a Bachelor's this is probably a good idea, considering that most data roles require a Bachelor's at a minimum (at least in prominent tech companies), but think twice if you've already got a Bachelor's. A Bachelor's degree in a seemingly irrelevant field (such as Communications) combined with a Master's in a technical field (like Data Science) will be more impactful than two Bachelor's degrees (one technical and one non-technical).

Also, if you're serious about pursuing another degree, it will be worth it to push yourself and take more rigorous coursework that goes along with post-graduate education. Lastly, it's likely that a Master's degree will actually take you less time than starting new Bachelor's program.

MasterTrack: Similarly to the MicroMasters from edX, this certificate carries a little extra weight simply because of the word, "Master's" in the description. Hiring teams will be at least a little more confident in your education background if they know your coursework was at the postgraduate level. Since there are no currently available offerings we won't be able to provide much detail, but go ahead and check in on the MasterTrack programs periodically and see if anything matches what you're looking for.

Cost

All-in costs with Coursera can vary greatly in both total amount and relative to other platforms, and we'll get into specifics here. One aspect worth mentioning up front is that the vast majority of content on Coursera can be accessed for free, and you can get the official certificate with a paid subscription. Coursera has (arguably) the most simple and easy-to-understand pricing of any of the platforms, and many feel it is the best value for the money. Let's dive in.

Individual Courses & Specializations: Since most individual courses are a part of a Specialization, the costs fall in line with each other. Whether you want to take a full Specialization program or just a single course, you'll have to enroll in the full Specialization and sign up for a monthly subscription, most of which are currently $49 per month (although they range from $40-$80 per monthly). Coursera offers a 7-day trial period before you're billed, and if you look around online you may be able to find some coupon codes that give you a discount or a longer unpaid period.

The great part about monthly subscriptions is that you only pay for as much time as it takes to complete the coursework. For example, the Specialization in Applied Data Science from the University of Michigan is estimated to take about 5 months to complete, which would be roughly $250 total. However, if you really want to put a ton of time into it every week and blitz through the material, you could knock it out in a month or two, taking your total cost for the specialization down to about $100. Not bad.

If you've invested in these chapters and are devoting time to learning the information we're teaching you, you're one of the few people who are motivated to break into the field of data and is willing to take action. Those who are motivated to put the work in love Coursera's subscription model because it motivates them to stay on top of their coursework and finish quickly, while still gaining mastery of the principles of successful data work. Compared to Udacity's $399 per month offer, Coursera's $49 per month subscription to be taught by top institutions is tough to beat.

Bachelor's & Master's Degrees: While degrees from Coursera are very valuable and fulfilling experiences, the pricing tends to be less competitive with other platforms offering degrees. The online Master's of Computer Science in Data Science from the University of Illinois will cost you around $22,000 for the whole program, while the Master's in Applied Data Science from the University of Michigan will cost an estimated $32,000-$42,000 as of the time of this writing. That's not exactly chump change. That said, these are top-tier universities, which is why they're able to command a higher tuition than other institutions.

MasterTrack: These small batches of post-graduate coursework are certainly less expensive than a full Master's, but are also above and beyond what you'd pay for a Specialization from Coursera. We don't have concrete information on what the costs will look like for data-oriented MasterTracks yet, but expect to pay somewhere in the neighborhood of $3,000-$5,000.

That's it. Two of Coursera's main strengths are its partnerships with top institutions and its highly-favored pricing model that incentivizes and rewards those who are willing to devote a concentrated effort to finishing courses or Specializations. Not to mention, even if you take the full estimated time to complete a Specialization, you'd be paying less than you would for similar certificates on other platforms.

Stepping Back

Hopefully the above has been helpful for you to understand the different online learning options in-depth, as well as the costs associated and various credentials available. Remember that, as we said in the beginning, we assumed that you've gone through "Self-Taught vs. Online: The Ultimate Guide" in order to figure out if online learning is right for you. If it is, this chapter on the top 3 online platforms will be a great resource in choosing the right online platform. In this section we're going to take a step back and look at the whole picture of what you're trying to accomplish, and ideally you'll be able to draw some conclusions that make sense of what can feel like a maze of really good options.

What is our outcome?

Your individual outcome is something juicy and personally motivating, like the example in the first section of this chapter: "My outcome is to create and cultivate top-level skills that help me get a fantastic job as a Data Scientist at a great company where I'd be excited to come into work every day". Overall we can say that our outcome is to get you a great job in the field of data. What defines "great" is up to you, but typically people talk about doing interesting work, working at a great company, and getting much better pay as reasons they want to break into this field. Whatever your reasons, make sure they're good ones and know that it is absolutely possible to make the leap if you're willing to put together a strategy (we'll help with that), invest in yourself (like you're doing with this chapter), and do the work.

Since we know our outcome, we need to think about things we can do to contribute to that outcome. We won't cover every detail here, but instead we'll focus on the parts that relate to online learning. Feel free to make a list of your own, but here's a start:

- Build skills relevant to the role you're interested in

- Learn concepts well enough to use on the job and to be successful

- Practice and be able to speak to the concepts or perform well in a whiteboard interview

It may sound overly simplistic, but the reason we're bringing this up is to reinforce the purpose of online coursework- to teach you the skills to get you where you want to be. Unfortunately many people start an online course, do a halfway decent job, and then stick it on their resume, which was the only reason they took the course in the first place. Online courses should be on your resume, but that's not the reason you're taking them.

So, why did we go through sections on credentialing for each platform in this chapter? While having the stamp on your resume is not the main focus, it is a fact that recruiters and hiring managers see that as a signal that you have the skills. If someone sees that you took graduate-level coursework in Data Science & Machine Learning from Harvard, it will have a bigger impact on their perception of you than if you put, "Self-Taught in Data Science and Machine Learning" on your resume- even if you have the same exact knowledge.

With this chapter we want to prepare you for two things: to have the skills necessary to get a job offer and succeed in the role, and to help you get a signal on your resume that will help you get an interview in the first place. The signal is important. It's very true that just because someone took some online courses, or even has a full Master's, from a place like Stanford doesn't mean they're inherently better than a candidate without those credentials.

But it's also true that recruiters and hiring managers look for signals like these to determine someone who is more likely to ultimately be a good fit for the role. This is why we've been nudging you in the direction of taking full online programs, particularly those sponsored by a brand-name institution.

We want to cover one more thing, and it may just save you a lot of money. Know this: you don't have to pay for a "Verified" certificate to put the coursework on your resume, and it may not actually matter whether or the program you completed could be verified. Remember that edX and Coursera both have options where you can take full programs for free, and only have to pay if you want a verified certificate.

In all likelihood, you won't need a verified certificate, and it's doubtful that many employers will ask or want to check. You could simply do the entire program and be honest about completing the assignments and checking your work, put the program on your resume, and on the rare chance the employer asks or wants to verify, you can just say, "Truthfully, I did the entire program and completed all the assignments, but I just decided not to pay for the certificate because I was mostly interested in learning the material and getting really good at the concepts. I'm happy to demonstrate any data concepts and undergo some additional technical interviews if you'd like".

What can they say to that? They'll probably say, "No, that's OK", or "Sure, let's do a few more coding challenges". If they say, "No, we don't believe you", then it's probably not a place you want to work anyway.

Do whatever makes you most comfortable. Some people like to go ahead and pay for the certificate because it makes them more motivated, while many just take the courses and add the program to your resume. As long as you're honest and don't say anything that's not true (eg. you have a Master's when you don't, etc.), you'll be fine.

Thoughts from a Hiring Manager

"Yes, we look at credentials. It's a little silly because I know and believe that people who went to brand-name schools aren't necessarily smarter or better at their jobs, but sometimes filtering resumes on those things helps our overall success rate. I like to see candidates that have done some additional coursework in Data Science, because it shows me that they're willing to put in the work.

I wouldn't go through any formal verification for online programs or certificates, but maybe that's just me. I definitely test all candidates for their skills in key concepts, and regardless of degrees or certificates I make sure they can display the knowledge needed to succeed in the role. I am also wary of people who exaggerate their abilities significantly. Everyone does this to an extent, but if you tell me that you're an "Expert" in Python and you can't write a simple loop, it's hard for me to see you as a legitimate candidate."

    That's about it for this chapter. Right now is an incredibly exciting time to get into the field of data because there are so many resources online, and much of it is available for free (or inexpensive). You can literally build a brand new, exciting career completely online. Remember that there are a lot of good options, and you don't have to choose the "perfect" one. Realistically, if you're willing to put in the effort, any of the above platforms (as well as many others) will get you in a place to earn a fantastic new role you'll love. The key is you and the effort you put in- many different approaches will work if you will.

www.ingramcontent.com/pod-product-compliance
Lightning Source LLC
Chambersburg PA
CBHW030538220526
45463CB00007B/2888